# It's Great to Be Grateful!

## A Kid's Guide to Being Thankful!

Written by Michaelene Mundy

Illustrated by R.W. Alley

ONE
CARING
PLACE

Abbey Press
St. Meinrad, IN 47577

Text © 2012 Michaelene Mundy
Illustrations © 2012 Saint Meinrad Archabbey
Published by One Caring Place
Abbey Press
St. Meinrad, Indiana 47577

Library of Congress Catalog Number
2012946114

ISBN 978-0-87029-512-6

# A Message to Parents, Teachers, and Other Caring Adults

We were raised to say "Please" and "Thank you," and we recognize the importance of passing these good manners on to our children. At the same time, we don't want these to be just words said without meaning. While helping the children in our lives "count the blessings" in their young lives, we can help them get into the habit of using the word "thanks" to make others happy, too.

As parents, we tend to give our children the *things* that we believe will make them happy. Because of our generosity, the opposite effect can take place. They can come to expect "things" and don't appreciate what they already have. We may see this especially at birthday and other holiday celebrations when a wanted gift is not received and the day is clouded because of it. That's when it hits home to us as caring adults that we need to teach our children the importance of truly feeling grateful and sharing that feeling with a "thank you."

We know how being on the receiving end of a "thank you" can make us feel. We appreciate that the person thanking us recognizes the time and effort put into some action or gift. Gratitude makes us happy. We want our children to be happy.

Writer David Steindl-Rast goes so far as to say, "It is not happiness that makes us grateful, but gratefulness that makes us happy." By helping children see the many things in their lives that they can be grateful for, we are helping them to be happy and to be able to handle times in their lives that are not so happy.

Another reason to be thankful is that our gratefulness makes *God* happy, too! The 13th century mystic, Meister Eckhart, is famously quoted as saying that "If the only prayer you said in your whole life was *'Thank you,'* that would suffice."

May this book provide you some help as you pass on to children good, lived lessons of appreciation and thankfulness!

—*Michaelene Mundy*

# What It Means to Be Grateful

Being grateful means you notice something good that has happened or is happening in your life. It might be something that just happened, like your mother fixing your favorite supper and it's not even your birthday.

When you take time to be thankful, ordinary things can become special: a cupcake tastes better if you slow down and enjoy it. Remembering that someone took the time to bake them is another reason to be grateful.

# Why Be Thankful?

It is hard to be thankful and sad—or angry—at the same time. Being thankful can make you feel good. Paying attention to the little things we have and the little things that happen can turn a boring day into a special day or an ordinary meal into a feast.

It is important to let others know when you are thankful for something they did for you or made happen. Even GOD likes to know when you are thankful. At the end of the day you can thank God for your family, your friends, or for things like snow that you had fun in.

# Being Thankful Is a Gift!

You "honor" or "show your respect" for someone when you notice them or what they do for you and then show or tell them that you are thankful with a smile or a hug and a "Thank you."

We can also hurt people's feelings by not being thankful. Did you ever do something special for someone—like holding the door open or carrying something for someone—and they didn't even notice? Did it make you feel sad?

It feels good when others say "Thanks" to you. It is like someone giving a gift to you.

# How to Be Thankful

You can show your thanks with a note, an e-mail, or a text. You can even stop the fun thing you are doing for a moment and whisper a thanks to God.

It isn't hard to be thankful. It does take a little time, though. It is a wonderful habit to notice when things are good and quietly say to yourself the feelings that are in your heart.

Sometimes we find it easier to say "Please," than "Thank you." We say "Please" when we are asking for good things we want for ourselves and for others. Saying "Thank you" can be every bit as important.

## To Whom Should We Give Thanks?

You can thank your mom and dad for the gift of your life. But you don't have to wait until your birthday. You can thank God for all the good people you have in your life–grandparents, friends, teachers, neighbors.

It is nice to show your thanks to people who take care of you or do little things for you. A friend who pushes you on a swing, your grandparent who takes care of you when your parents are gone, your teachers who help you learn new things, the librarian who helps you find a good book, are all people to whom we can say "Thank you."

There are so many people to thank!

# What to Be Thankful For

There are a million things to be grateful for. Things like your family and good meals to eat together. You can be thankful for a summer breeze on a hot day, or for the toys and games you have.

But you probably don't really need more and more stuff. Instead, you can be thankful for the things and people you have in your life. And you can be thankful that you have people who love you and watch over you. These are the best gifts and blessings in your life.

# Being Thankful Is a Choice

Being thankful sometimes just happens and is easy to show. When someone surprises you with something nice, you may smile or jump up and down or give a big hug or say, "Thanks!"

But sometimes, showing gratitude and saying "thanks" is a choice. It is something you can decide to do. As a child, you get lots of help and things done for you. It is easy to take some of these things for granted. Your mother may bring you a cool glass of lemonade when you are playing outside on a hot day. A big brother or sister may help you put on boots to go play in the snow. Letting them know you appreciate them means a lot. Make showing gratitude a habit.

## Make a List

List the things that make you happy, the things that you are grateful for. Write them down or have someone write them down for you.

A favorite game, a special friend, or even ice cream will probably show up on everyone's list! What about being thankful for your hands and your feet? Think of the wonderful things you can hold and the places you can go and the amazing things in the world that you get to see and touch and hear.

Think of the things around you that make life good and you can be thankful for—like flowers and trees, clean air to breathe, pure water to drink, a soft bed to sleep in, enough food to eat, a good book to read, caring people.

# When to Be Thankful

Every single day of your life there are many things to be thankful for!

A wise person long ago said that we need only three things to be happy, three things to be really thankful for: something to do, someone to love, and something to look forward to. Today, what is the something to do that you are thankful for, who is there for you to love and be thankful for, and what are you looking forward to that makes you thankful?

If you can name something for the three things above, you are lucky; you are blessed. It is good to be thankful in our hearts. It is good to say it out loud. Saying, "Thanks" for the blessings in your life is something you can keep doing all of your life. Make it a habit—something that you do automatically.

# Grateful for Things We Can't Even See!

There are many wonderful things to be thankful for that you cannot see. Many of these "invisible" things are some of the best things in your life.

You can be grateful for some things that you can only feel in your heart: things like God's love for you, or that your family and friends still love you after you make mistakes, or that your grandparent knows just when you are ready for a snack.

# Sometimes It's Hard to Be Thankful

It's easy to be thankful for some things—like presents, good health, sunshine, a new little puppy, or a baby sister or brother.

At other times, it can be very hard to be thankful—like when the present wasn't what you hoped for, when your baby brother or sister gets all the attention, or when your new puppy keeps barking too much and you can't sleep.

Sometimes it's hard to be thankful for things like rain—especially during a picnic or a ballgame. And then there are dentists and doctors that give shots and yucky medicines. But you need all of these people and things, too. You can be grateful when they help you be well and have a nice smile.

## Make It a Habit to Say "Thank You"

You may hear people say, "Thank goodness we have air conditioning," or, "Thank heavens I passed that test," or "Thank God no one got hurt." Being thankful is such a habit with some people that they often don't even realize they are doing it.

Getting into the habit of saying "Thank you" to God is a very good thing. And it is also a very good habit to say "Thanks" for all the good and kind things people do.

When you notice someone being kind, tell them so. It can make their whole day special to know that you noticed.

# We Also Need to Care and Share

If you become more thankful for people and all of creation, you will also become more caring. It also means you will want to keep things nice for yourself and others.

For example, when you get a new toy or game or pet that you are very thankful for, you naturally want to take good care of the toy or the pet.

The same is true when you start noticing more and more how beautiful the many parts of our world are. Then you will want to take better and better care of the Earth and all that we have on it.

# Every Day Can Be a Thanksgiving Day!

Have you ever heard someone say, "Count your blessings"? People often say this when bad things happen. By looking at the good things in your life, it makes it easier to deal with bad things that happen sometimes.

At night, before sleep, when all is quiet, (except for maybe your little brother or sister or puppy!) remember to tell God how thankful you are… thankful for all that was, all that is, and all that will be.

**Michaelene Mundy** has written many popular books for children, including *Sometimes I'm Afraid—A Book About Fear*, for the *Just for Me Books* series by Abbey Press. She has also written *Sad Isn't Bad* and *Mad Isn't Bad* for the Abbey Press *Elf-help for Kids book* series. She is a counselor and mother residing in Jasper, Indiana.

**R. W. Alley** is the illustrator for the popular Abbey Press adult series of Elf-help books, as well as an illustrator and writer of children's books. He lives in Barrington, Rhode Island, with his wife, daughter, and son. See a wide variety of his works at: www.rwalley.com.